small wonders

Tiny Treasures to Fuse, Embroider, and Enjoy

SERENA BOFFA SODA

Martingale®
Create with Confidence

Small Wonders: Tiny Treasures to Fuse, Embroider, and Enjoy
© 2018 by Serena Boffa Soda

Martingale®
19021 120th Ave. NE, Ste. 102
Bothell, WA 98011-9511 USA
ShopMartingale.com

Printed in China
23 22 21 20 19 18   8 7 6 5 4 3 2 1

Library of Congress Cataloging-in-Publication Data
is available upon request.

ISBN: 978-1-60468-892-4

MISSION STATEMENT

We empower makers who use fabric and yarn
to make life more enjoyable.

CREDITS

PUBLISHER AND
CHIEF VISIONARY OFFICER
Jennifer Erbe Keltner

CONTENT DIRECTOR
Karen Costello Soltys

DESIGN MANAGER
Adrienne Smitke

MANAGING EDITOR
Tina Cook

PRODUCTION MANAGER
Regina Girard

ACQUISITIONS EDITOR
Karen M. Burns

PHOTOGRAPHER
Brent Kane

TECHNICAL EDITOR
Nancy Mahoney

ILLUSTRATOR
Christine Erikson

COPY EDITOR
Melissa Bryan

DEDICATION

*Thank you to my family, made up of
talented people with golden hands.*

*Thanks to my mom, Liliana, for teaching me
without limits; you gave me big wings to fly high.*

Thanks to my husband, Ivo; you put the wind under those wings.

*Thanks to my sweet friend Anne; you are
the most generous person I have ever met.*

*Last, but not least . . . to Dad; I know
you are proud of me in Heaven.*

I love you all!

contents

Bonus Project Online!
Visit ShopMartingale.com/SmallWonders
to download Into the Wild for free.

introduction

─────────── ♡ ───────────

I love the little things. In little things reside the most precious details, those finely crafted with love, those that you don't notice at first glance but that end up making all the difference. This was the starting point as I searched for the *leitmotif*—the recurring theme—for this book. When I added my love of the outdoors and the beauty of breathtaking sceneries that Mother Nature generously gives us, the answer became obvious. I just had to go with my mind to the amazing views of my homeland, Italy, or to faraway places I've had the chance to visit, and by doing so, I found the perfect subjects to translate into real projects. This book is dedicated to the simple life, pulsing with slow, cozy rhythms and marked by the harmony of nature—an "old-style" life that today's modernity has overshadowed. In this world, everything is made small but with great attention to every possible detail, because the details matter the most. It's the details and the love we put into them that transform the ordinary into the extraordinary. The silent landscapes come alive with glimpses of daily life, like little red-roofed houses, clothes hung out to dry, or a tractor ready to harvest pumpkins.

After giving life to the creations in *Small Wonders,* my second priority was to create a book that was not limited to only the projects included, but that would give the creative reader the opportunity to interchange blocks. Therefore, I deliberately made all the blocks the same size so that they can be "transplanted" easily from one project to another. One book, four projects, endless combinations.

To reproduce these miniature creations, you just need basic sewing and embroidery knowledge, patience, and lots of love. I invite you to take your time and, as Mother Teresa of Calcutta wisely said, "Do small things with great love."

My little world is ready to greet and pamper you. Welcome!

~ Serena

materials and tools

The right materials and tools can make life easier, help you achieve great results, and make the pursuit of your creative passion even more pleasant!

MATERIALS

The following are my favorite materials that I used for the projects in this book.

Cotton fabrics. I recommend prewashing cotton fabrics (see "Preparing Fabrics" on page 7) to ensure colorfastness.

Threads. I primarily use two different kinds of 100% cotton threads in my projects. Aurifil 50-weight thread is perfect for machine piecing and joining English-paper-piecing shapes. When appliquéing by hand, I choose a finer-weight option, such as Aurifil 80-weight thread, for each step from finishing fusible-appliqué shapes to sewing English-paper-pieced compositions onto the background piece. This thread is as fine as silk and blends perfectly into fabrics. Basting thread comes in handy, too, for English paper piecing and for thread basting a quilt sandwich prior to hand quilting.

Embroidery floss. My favorite embroidery floss is 6-strand cotton floss by Valdani, because it's available in the largest, most beautiful palette of variegated colors. It has a matte finish, and since it's variegated, you don't need to change threads for a shaded effect as you do when using solid colors. I love Valdani's wool thread as well—rustic and fluffy, it gives extra texture to details compared to cotton floss. When using either thread, work with a short length to prevent breakage.

Lightweight fusible stabilizer. A lightweight fusible stabilizer is a must-have. I use one recommended for use on silks in dressmaking. Fuse it under your fabrics before doing any embroidery or appliqué. It will help achieve a smooth, wrinkle-free surface without making the fabric too stiff.

Fusible web. Without fusible web, I couldn't create such small appliqué details, because it would be too difficult to needle turn the tiny edges. I prefer HeatnBond Ultrahold because the two adhesive sides stick to both the background fabric and the appliqué shapes, aiding in placing the appliqués. For the tiny details in this book, I highly recommend a heavyweight fusible web. You'll be using such small pieces of it that there's no need to worry about them stiffening the project, and the heavier weight will help prevent fraying.

Water-soluble appliqué paper. I love this paper for turned-edge appliqué and English paper piecing; it helps maintain the perfect shape while I'm working. Just as you would with freezer paper, trace shapes onto the nonadhesive side of the paper. Then fuse the adhesive side to the wrong side of the fabric with a warm iron. Unlike freezer paper, appliqué paper is water soluble, so it will disappear after the first washing, leaving your piece quite soft.

Fusible fleece. My secret weapon when I need dimension is fleece that's fusible on one side. My favorite is Floriani's Heat N Sta fusible fleece, which is stable, soft, and maintains its shape perfectly after pressing while keeping its loft. Learn how I use fusible fleece in "English Paper Piecing" (page 12).

Preparing Fabrics

I use only premium 100% cotton quilting fabrics. To give life to my teeny-tiny appliqué details, I choose small-scale prints for their subtle impact. Despite my creative rush when I buy new fabrics, I always gently prewash them before use. I do this for two reasons: Fabrics can shrink, and colors can bleed. Here's how I prewash my fabrics:

1. Divide the fabrics by color and soak them in cold water.

2. Rinse and change the water several times. When the water is clear and the dyes are set, add a cup of white vinegar and rinse one more time.

3. Let the fabrics dry in the open air, but don't squeeze them or you may create unpleasant creases. Press the fabrics when they're still damp to remove wrinkles.

Even if you've spent time prewashing your fabrics, use a color-catcher sheet for the first two machine washings. Better safe than sorry!

Batting. I used a thick polyester batting for all the projects in this book. It doesn't need to be prewashed, keeps its shape perfectly, and provides a strong hold for wall hangings and table toppers. It's also beautiful once quilted.

Tape. You can use transparent tape, painter's tape, or washi tape to secure your patterns to a light source for tracing.

Buttons. I love collecting and using buttons! Whether new or vintage, tiny or big, buttons add a quick and easy extra touch. Buttons are easy to find in quilting, craft, and fabric stores, but if you really need something special to add to a project, antique buttons are the answer with their old-fashioned style. The best place to look for distinctive buttons is in Grandma's or Mom's drawers and cabinets—you may find jars full of little gems! Keep your eyes open when poking around yard sales or flea markets, as well, because you could find a treasure just waiting for you.

TOOLS

The right tools are as important as the right materials. Using the proper tool will save you precious time and effort, ensuring a more enjoyable and rewarding sewing experience.

Sewing machine and accessories. You don't need an expensive sewing machine to sew with love. It must be reliable with a strong motor and be able to sew through the layers efficiently during the most demanding process—machine quilting. Take care of your sewing machine and schedule regular cleanings. If you machine quilt, a walking foot is a must to prevent puckers. If you love to finish your raw appliqué edges by machine, an open-toe foot is another great tool to own. A free-motion or darning foot is also essential for any free-motion quilting.

Rotary-cutting tools. A rotary cutter, cutting mat, and acrylic rulers will speed up the cutting process. I use a 6" × 24" ruler for larger pieces and squaring up quilt tops. An 8½"-square ruler is good for cutting small pieces and trimming block backgrounds to the perfect size.

Iron and Teflon pressing sheets. An iron is your best friend, and lately I have learned not to be afraid of using steam. Very gentle steam can be quite helpful when pressing seams. Pressing sheets are great, especially when adhering fusible web or fusible fleece to the back of fabric shapes. For this process, hold the iron to the project surface slightly longer than usual; a pressing sheet will prevent fabric from scorching or adhesive from sticking to the surface of your iron.

Light box. If you want the perfect tool for transferring patterns, treat yourself to a light box. But if investing in a light box isn't an option, a daylight window is a great free resource.

Markers. I use a variety of marking tools. For light fabrics, I mostly use a FriXion pen by Pilot, because the marks disappear with heat from an iron. While a FriXion pen works great on light fabrics, I use it sparingly on darker fabrics because, although the marks disappear, they tend to leave a white "ghost" mark. Instead, I use a white chalk pencil on dark fabrics. The chalk mark is clearly visible and it disappears with a simple rub. I'm not a great fan of water-soluble markers, because I've had trouble getting the marks to disappear completely. If you use a water-soluble marker, use it lightly, and never pass twice over the same mark. I also use a black Pigma pen, size 01, to add some very small details to projects and to personalize the labels when I sign my creations.

Scissors and seam rippers. You'll need several types of scissors. The most important is a good pair of fabric scissors. Use them only for cutting fabric, or the blade will become dulled or damaged. Utility scissors are needed for preparing templates or cutting fusible shapes for appliqué. A pair of small embroidery scissors with pointed tips is helpful for cutting little shapes. And then, of course, we all need a seam ripper from time to time.

Pins and needles. Pins are essential for achieving perfect matches. Straight, fine pins with glass or plastic heads are easy to find, so use them. Use a good, sharp needle for all appliqué. Use a crewel needle with a sharp point and elongated eye for embroidery. Safety pins are helpful when basting the quilt sandwich before machine quilting.

Water-soluble fabric glue pen. When it comes to English paper piecing, I couldn't live without a glue pen. The glue is colored so that you can easily see where you're putting it, but it dries clear (and quickly) in the air.

techniques

All you need to start working on the projects in this book is a knowledge of some fundamental quiltmaking techniques and basic embroidery skills.

TRANSFERRING PATTERNS

The easiest way to transfer patterns is by using a light source. I treated myself to a light box, which has been the best purchase ever! If you don't own a light box, a well-lit window (or even a tablet screen) will work.

Light Fabrics

You'll have more stitching success if you stabilize fabrics before you embroider or appliqué. However, because the marks of a FriXion pen disappear under heat, be sure to stabilize your fabric *before* transferring your design so that you won't lose the transfer lines. Tape the pattern to your light source. Place the stabilized fabric on top and secure it too. Trace the pattern using a FriXion pen. Note that the appliqué patterns are reversed for fusible appliqué, but the embroidery patterns are not reversed. They appear as they will be in the final project.

Remember, don't press the project until the appliqué or embroidery work is completed, or you will lose the traced markings. If this happens, you'll need to transfer the design again.

Dark or Opaque Fabrics

Light sources don't work for tracing onto dark or opaque fabrics. In these situations, I use the following process.

1. Trace the pattern onto parchment paper. Use a pin to make evenly spaced holes along the traced lines.

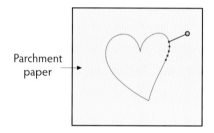

Parchment paper →

2. Pin the parchment-paper pattern on top of the fabric. Using a white chalk pencil and going through the holes in the pattern, mark the design on the underlying fabric. If the fabric is light, but opaque, use a FriXion pen instead of a white chalk pencil.

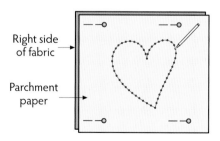

Right side of fabric →

Parchment paper →

3. Remove the parchment-paper pattern and connect the dots using a chalk pencil or marker.

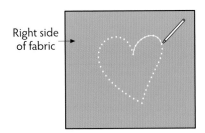

Right side of fabric →

FUSIBLE APPLIQUÉ

I use heavyweight fusible web for tiny appliqués to keep the raw edges from fraying. If you haven't already found the perfect fusible web, ask at your local quilt shop for recommendations.

Manufacturer's instructions vary for different fusible products. Generally speaking, however, I follow these steps.

1. Trace the pattern onto the paper side of the fusible web. Roughly cut out the shapes, leaving a ⅛" to ¼" margin all around the marked line.

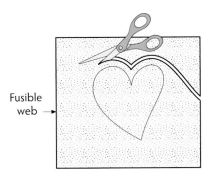

Fusible web →

2. Place the shapes, fusible side down, on the wrong side of the appropriate appliqué fabric. Follow the manufacturer's instructions to fuse the shapes to the fabric, and let the shapes cool. Lay something heavy (a book works great) on the fused shapes to be sure the hot adhesive sticks securely to the entire surface. When cool, cut out the fabric shapes exactly on the drawn lines. Wait to peel off the paper backing until you're ready to use the fabric shape; otherwise, the fabric tends to curl, making placement more difficult.

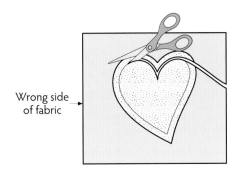

Wrong side of fabric →

3. Place the appliqué shapes, adhesive side down, on the right side of the background fabric and press. Press again from the wrong side. Then allow the appliqué to cool, again placing a weight on top.

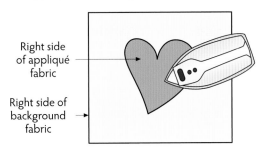

Right side of appliqué fabric →

Right side of background fabric →

4. When all the pieces have been fused in place, whipstitch around the raw edges (see page 15) to secure the appliqués to the background fabric. Using perfectly matched thread will make the stitches disappear.

ENGLISH PAPER PIECING

English paper piecing, or EPP, is relaxing and fun. It's very accurate and is a great take-along project.

English paper piecing involves folding fabric over templates and then hand sewing the prepared shapes together. The templates ensure that the shapes are accurate and easy to piece.

For the projects in this book, you'll be working with templates made from three different materials: cardstock, water-soluble appliqué paper, and fusible fleece. Each one will allow you to achieve a different finished look.

The projects are composed of different shapes, including apple cores, hexagons, petals, and elongated hexagons. Follow these general instructions to make a template.

1. Trace the shape onto the template material the number of times indicated on the pattern. Cut out the shapes on the drawn line. Use a light source when tracing onto cardstock or appliqué paper. When using fusible fleece, trace the shape onto cardstock first. Then place the cardstock template on the fluffy side of the fusible fleece and use a permanent marker to trace around the template.

2. Choose your fabric and refer to the steps in the following sections, according to which template material you're using.

Cardstock Template

1. Use a hole punch to create a small opening in the center of the cardstock template. Simply pin through the center of the hole as shown, without piercing the paper.

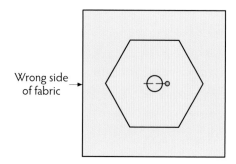

Wrong side of fabric →

2. Use a ruler to mark a ¼"-wide seam allowance around the shape. Use sharp scissors to cut out the shape on the marked line.

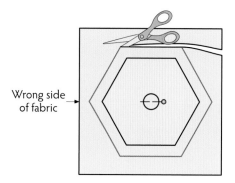

Wrong side of fabric →

3. Fold the seam allowance over the template. Using regular sewing thread, stitch through the folded corners of the fabric to hold it around the paper. Don't stitch through the template. Press to mark the folds.

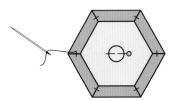

Appliqué-Paper Template

1. Place the paper template on the wrong side of the fabric, shiny side down. Following the manufacturer's instructions, fuse the layers.

2. Use a ruler to mark a ⅜"-wide seam allowance around the template. Use sharp scissors to cut out the shape on the marked line.

3. Apply a line of fabric glue on the template near the edge. Fold the seam allowance over the template onto the glue line and hold until secured. Repeat for all seam allowances. Press to mark the fold. The fabric glue and appliqué paper will dissolve in the first washing.

Glue
line

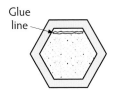

Fusible-Fleece Template

1. Place the fleece template on the wrong side of the fabric, shiny side down. Follow the manufacturer's instructions to fuse the layers. It's important to press in an up-and-down motion, as sliding the iron from side to side may cause the fleece to distort and lose its original shape.

2. Use a ruler to mark a ⅜"-wide seam allowance around the template. Use sharp scissors to cut out the shape on the marked line.

3. Fold the seam allowance over the template. Using basting thread, stitch around the shape, sewing through all the layers to secure the seam allowances. Knot the thread on the right side of the shape so it can be removed easily. Be very careful with this step, and always compare the prepared shape to the original cardstock template to maintain the correct shape and size.

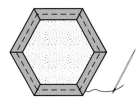

Assembling the Shapes

Once you've prepared all the shapes required, you're ready to assemble them. The classic stitch for joining English-paper-piecing shapes is a whipstitch. But you may find that the ladder stitch works better. Use a sharp, thin needle, and always choose matching thread to make the stitches practically disappear.

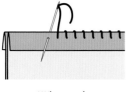 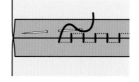

Whipstitch   Ladder stitch

I use the following technique for joining most English-paper-pieced units, such as hexagons, petals, and elongated hexagons. For apple cores, you'll find additional instructions with the project.

While sewing shapes together, take care not to stitch too deep into the fabric. Instead, let the stitches run along the folded seam allowances. This makes the difference between a visible stitch and an invisible stitch on the front of your project.

1. Lay out all the pieces for a block.

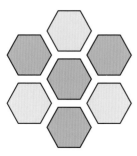

2. Place the first two pieces you want to join right sides together. Make a couple of stitches in one corner to secure the thread.

3. Sew along one side, taking stitches that are not too close together. As you work, pull on the thread to tighten the stitches, being careful to avoid any puckering. You'll achieve the right stitch distance and tension as you gain more practice.

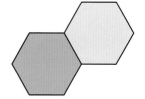

4. Stitch all the seams to assemble the block, knotting the thread at each corner or intersection, even if you're going to continue sewing onto the next piece. Make a knot at the intersection, but don't clip the thread. To travel to an unstitched side, sew a running stitch in the seam allowance only. Knot the thread and then stitch the next side seam.

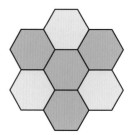 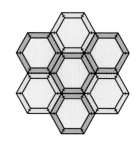

Once the blocks are complete, stitch them to the background fabric using a blind stitch. If you've used cardstock templates, you'll need to remove the templates before attaching the block to the background. Appliqué-paper and fusible-fleece templates do not need to be removed.

EMBROIDERY

Embroidery gives a project the finishing touch that makes a world of difference, which is why I love using it in my pieces. Even basic easy stitches add interesting textures and detail. All of the embroidery stitches are worked using one or two strands of floss, as indicated in each project.

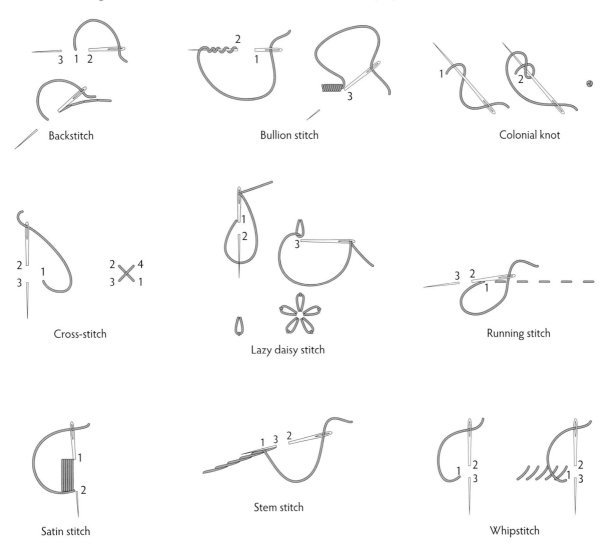

Backstitch

Bullion stitch

Colonial knot

Cross-stitch

Lazy daisy stitch

Running stitch

Satin stitch

Stem stitch

Whipstitch

four seasons dream
wall hanging

I've always been fascinated by the magic of the four seasons, each having its own individual "personality" and unique color scheme. In this wall hanging, I've tried to capture the essence of spring, summer, fall, and winter in three-dimensional central medallions embellished with tiny hand-embroidered details.

FINISHED WALL HANGING: 24½" × 24½"
FINISHED BLOCKS: 8" × 8"

MATERIALS

Yardage is based on 42"-wide fabric. Fat eighths measure 9" × 21".

Fabrics

⅓ yard of cream solid for block backgrounds

½ yard of ecru tone on tone for border

4 fat eighths of assorted blue prints for skies

2 fat eighths of different green prints for hills

1 fat eighth of white print for snow-covered hills

1 fat eighth of orange print for field

5" × 7" rectangle of gold print for corner elongated hexagons

3" × 5" rectangle of yellow print for center elongated hexagons

Assorted scraps for buildings, clouds, clothing, truck, moon, and snowman appliqués

⅓ yard of red-and-purple gingham for small hexagons and binding

⅞ yard of fabric for backing

Blocks are shown at actual size on pages 26–29.

Other Materials

29" × 29" square of batting

10" × 20" rectangle of fusible fleece

3" × 15" rectangle of paper-backed fusible web

4 vintage cream buttons, ⅜" diameter

2 brown micro buttons, about ⅛" diameter

3 jet Swarovski flat-back rhinestones, 1.5 mm

6 crystal Swarovski flat-back rhinestones, 2 mm

Glue pen

Black Pigma pen, size 01

Cardstock

Wool Thread

Colors listed are for Valdani wool thread.

Black (W111), size 15, for sheep tails, ears,
and heads

Ivory (W400), size 8, for sheep bodies

Ivory (W400), size 15, for snowballs

Cotton Embroidery Floss

Colors listed are for 6-strand Valdani embroidery floss.

Black Medium (8112) for sheep legs

Brown (P12) for clothesline stakes, fences,
swing seat, flower centers, pumpkin stems,
and snowman arms

Copper Leaf (M78) for leaves

Distant Grass (M80) for leaves and hilly line

Heavenly Hue (JP11) for chimney smoke
and truck window

Icy Leaves (O565) for pathway and leaves

Nantucket Rose (JP5) for petals

Old Cottage Grey (O126) for chimneys, clothesline,
clothespins, birds, windows, roof, swing ropes,
weather vane, truck bumpers, and cross

Olive Green (P2) for grass, flower stems, and leaves

Quiet Fall (O534) for pumpkins and snowman nose

Rich Wine (O507) for apples, tower roof, and
snowman scarf

Rust (H201) for tree trunks, branches, and pathway

Rusty Gold (O67) for petals, hilly line, and pathway

Spring Lights (M12) for flower centers, truck
headlight, and windows

Subtle Elegance (M49) for doorway, windows,
hilly line, and hill accents

Tea-Dyed Stone (O178) for flower stems
and hilly line

Toffee (O505) for doors

CUTTING

From the cream solid, cut:

4 squares, 8½" × 8½"

From the ecru tone on tone, cut:

3 strips, 4½" × 42"; crosscut into:
    2 strips, 4½" × 16½"
    2 strips, 4½" × 24½"

From the red-and-purple gingham, cut:

3 strips, 2½" × 42"

PREPARING THE APPLIQUÉS

Refer to "Fusible Appliqué" on page 11 as needed. Appliqué patterns and their respective medallion patterns appear on pages 66–69.

1. Trace each appliqué shape once onto the paper side of the fusible web. Roughly cut out the fusible-web shapes.

2. Place each shape, fusible side down, on the wrong side of the appropriate appliqué fabric. Follow the manufacturer's instructions to fuse the shapes to the fabric. Let the fused shapes cool, and then carefully cut them out on the drawn lines. Wait to peel off the paper backing until you're ready to use the fabric shape.

MAKING THE TEMPLATES

1. Using the patterns on page 70, trace one large hexagon and one petal onto cardstock. Cut out the templates exactly on the traced lines.

2. Use the templates to trace four large hexagons and 24 petals onto the nonadhesive side of the fusible fleece.

3. Carefully cut out each shape on the traced line to avoid distortion. Check the shapes against the original pattern for accuracy.

Fusible fleece

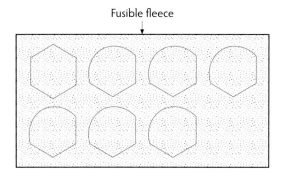

4. Using the medallion patterns, trace the horizontal center row (one hexagon and two petals) of each medallion onto cardstock, including the hilly line. Cut out the three shapes. The shapes cover the movement of the hills.

5. Cut each shape on the hilly line to separate the hills from the sky. Set aside, making sure to keep the shapes from each medallion together.

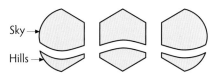

Sky

Hills

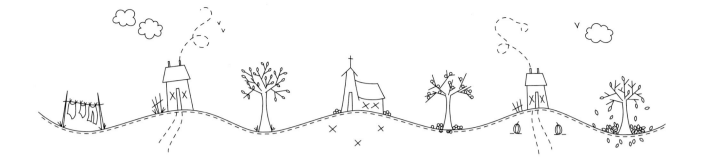

PREPARING THE PLAIN SHAPES

1. Using the cardstock templates, trace two petals for the sky onto the wrong side of one blue print. Trace two petals for the hills onto the wrong side of one green print. Cut out the petals, adding a ⅜"-wide seam allowance all around each shape. If using a directional print, pay attention to the orientation of the print.

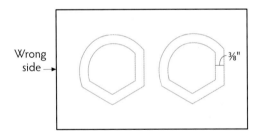

2. Center a fusible-fleece shape, adhesive side down, on the wrong side of each fabric shape. Following the manufacturer's instructions, fuse the layers.

3. Repeat steps 1 and 2 using the remaining blue, green, white, and orange prints to prepare two sky and two hill shapes for each medallion.

PREPARING THE COMPLEX SHAPES

Work on one medallion at a time, starting with Spring. Repeat the instructions to prepare the shapes for all four medallions.

1. Trace two petals and one hexagon onto the wrong side of one blue fat eighth. Cut out the shapes, adding a ⅜"-wide seam allowance all around each shape. If using a directional print, pay attention to the orientation of the print.

2. Using the medallion pattern and a light source, trace the outer sewing line and the hilly line onto the right side of the hexagon and both petal-fabric shapes. Set aside.

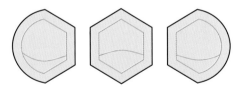

3. Place the cardstock hill templates right side down on the wrong side of a green fat eighth. Trace and cut out the shapes, adding a ⅜"-wide seam allowance all around the shapes.

4. Clip the upper seam allowances of the three fabric hill shapes, stopping a few threads before the traced lines. Clipping makes it easier to fold the seam allowance over the template.

5. Reposition each cardstock hill template on the wrong side of the corresponding green fabric shapes. Finger-press the clipped seam allowance over the template. Press to set the fold, and remove the cardstock template.

6. Glue a concave hill on each petal shape from step 2, placing the edge of the hill shape on the traced line. Appliqué the hills in place. Do not press, as it may cause the traced outline to fade. The outline is still needed as a placement guideline.

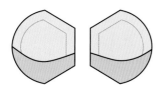

7. On the hexagon shape, appliqué the building before adding the fabric hill. The bottom edge of the building sits slightly below the traced convex hilly line. Once the building is attached, repeat step 6 to appliqué the hill in place. If any mark disappears during the fusible-appliqué process, trace the line again, as it's still needed for placement guidance. All the doors will be embroidered later, except for the barn doors of the Summer medallion, which need to be appliquéd along with the body of the building.

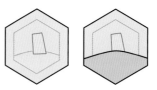

8. Working from the wrong side, trim away the excess blue fabric under the hills, leaving a ⅜" seam allowance on the back of each shape.

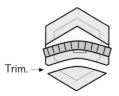

Trim. →

9. Using a light source, center the remaining fusible-fleece shapes within the traced outline on the back of the corresponding fabric shapes. Fuse the layers.

ASSEMBLING THE MEDALLIONS

1. Referring to "English Paper Piecing" on page 12, use a ladder stitch to join the shapes, sewing one side at a time and making sure to maintain the original dimensions. Always check the shapes against the original patterns for accuracy. Knot, but don't clip, the thread at each corner. To travel to an unstitched side, sew a running stitch in the seam allowance only. Knot the thread and then ladder stitch the next side seam.

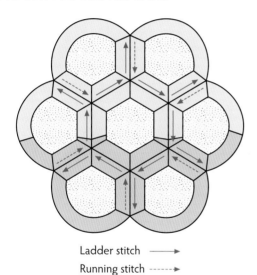

Ladder stitch ⟶
Running stitch ----▶

2. Remove all basting thread on the interior section of the medallions before beginning the additional appliqué and embroidery work. Keep the basting thread around the outer edges only.

Spring Medallion

Referring to the Spring medallion pattern, appliqué the roof and clouds. Embroider the clothesline and then appliqué the hanging clothes. All embroidery is stitched using two strands of cotton floss unless otherwise noted.

- **Satin stitch:** door in Toffee and tree trunk in Rust

- **Stem stitch:** clothesline stakes in Brown

- **Backstitch:** chimneys in Old Cottage Grey; branches in Rust; fence in Brown; clothesline, clothespins, and birds in one strand of Old Cottage Grey; grass in one strand of Olive Green; and flower stems in Tea-Dyed Stone

- **Running stitch:** hilly line in Tea-Dyed Stone, smoke from chimney in one strand of Heavenly Hue, and pathway in one strand of Rust

- **Cross-stitch:** windows in Old Cottage Grey

- **Lazy daisy stitch:** leaves in Distant Grass

- **Colonial knot:** flower centers in Spring Lights and petals in Nantucket Rose

Summer Medallion

Referring to the Summer medallion pattern, appliqué the clouds. Mark the window rectangles on the doorway with a black Pigma pen. All embroidery is stitched using two strands of cotton floss unless otherwise noted.

- **Satin stitch:** tree trunk in Rust

- **Stem stitch:** roof in Old Cottage Grey

- **Backstitch:** fence and swing seat in Brown; swing ropes, weather vane, and birds in one strand of Old Cottage Grey; flower stems and grass in one strand of Olive Green; and sheep legs in Black Medium

- **Running stitch:** hilly line in Distant Grass and pathway in one strand of Icy Leaves

- **Cross-stitch:** doorway and window in Subtle Elegance

- **Lazy daisy stitch:** petals in one strand of Rusty Gold; leaves in one strand of Olive Green; and sheep tails and ears in Black wool, size 15

- **Colonial knot:** leaves in Icy Leaves; apples in Rich Wine; flower centers in Brown; sheep bodies in Ivory wool, size 8; and sheep heads in Black wool, size 15

Fall Medallion

Referring to the Fall medallion pattern, appliqué the roof, truck, and clouds. All embroidery is stitched using two strands of cotton floss unless otherwise noted.

- **Satin stitch:** door in Toffee and tree trunk in Rust

- **Backstitch:** chimneys and truck bumpers in Old Cottage Grey, fence and pumpkin stems in Brown, branches in Rust, and birds in one strand of Old Cottage Grey

- **Running stitch:** hilly line in Rusty Gold, smoke in one strand of Heavenly Hue, and pathway in one strand of Rusty Gold

- **Cross-stitch:** windows in Old Cottage Grey and truck window in Heavenly Hue

- **Lazy daisy stitch:** leaves in one strand of Copper Leaf

- **Bullion stitch:** truck headlight in Spring Lights and pumpkins in Quiet Fall

- Attach the micro buttons for the truck wheels.

Winter Medallion

Referring to the Winter medallion pattern, appliqué the roof, snowman body, and moon. Use a black Pigma pen to mark the round window in the tower and the snowman's eyes. All embroidery is stitched using two strands of cotton floss unless otherwise noted.

- **Satin stitch:** door in Toffee and tree trunk in Rust

- **Backstitch:** roof of the tower in Rich Wine, cross in Old Cottage Grey, snowman arms in Brown, snowman nose in Quiet Fall, and branches in Rust

- **Running stitch:** hilly line in Subtle Elegance and outline the moon using one strand of floss similar to the fabric color

- **Cross-stitch:** windows in Spring Lights and hill accents in Subtle Elegance

- **Stem stitch:** snowman scarf in Rich Wine

- **Colonial knot:** snowballs in Ivory wool, size 15

- Following the manufacturer's instructions, hot fix the jet Swarovski flat-back rhinestones as snowman buttons and the crystal Swarovski flat-back rhinestones as falling snow.

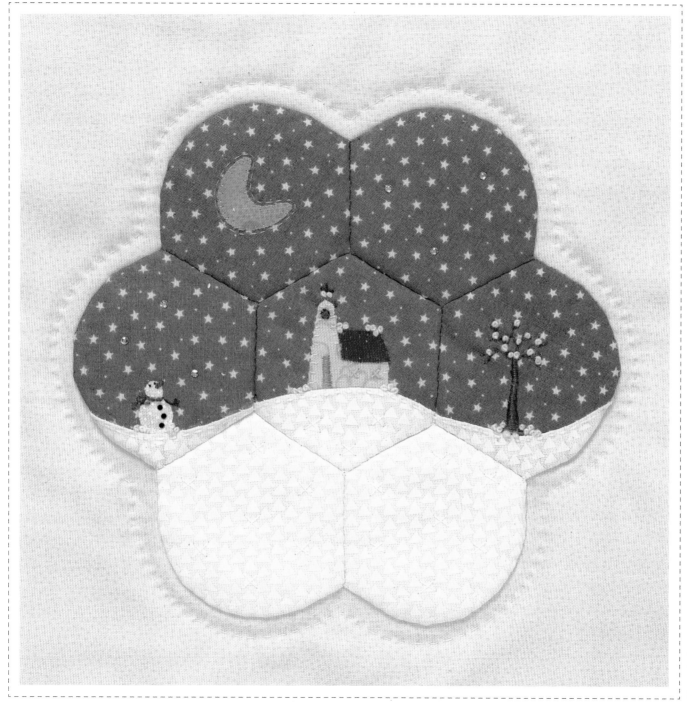

ASSEMBLING THE WALL HANGING

Press the seam allowances in the directions
indicated by the arrows.

1. Center and appliqué each decorated medallion
on a cream square to complete four blocks that
measure 8½" square, including the seam
allowances.

Make 4 blocks,
8½" × 8½".

2. Lay out the blocks in two rows of two blocks
each as shown in the assembly diagram. Sew the
blocks in each row together. Join the rows to make
the wall-hanging center, which should measure
16½" square, including the seam allowances.

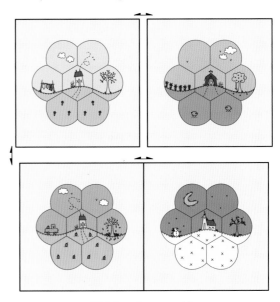

Wall-hanging assembly

3. Sew the ecru 16½"-long strips to the top and
bottom of the wall-hanging center. Sew the ecru
24½"-long strips to the sides of the wall hanging
to complete the border. Press all seam allowances
toward the center. The wall hanging should
measure 24½" square.

FINISHING THE WALL HANGING

For more detailed information about any finishing steps, visit ShopMartingale.com/HowtoQuilt.

1. Cut the backing fabric 4" larger than the wall-hanging top. Layer the top with batting and backing. Baste the layers together.

2. Machine or hand quilt. I quilted in the ditch along the intersecting seams of the center squares, around and very close to the four medallions, and around the perimeter of the wall-hanging center. A decorative running stitch was used around the medallions, about ¼" from the seamline. Four concentric squares were echo quilted all around the perimeter of the wall-hanging center, with the lines spaced about ½" apart.

3. Square up the quilt sandwich.

4. Use the gingham 2½"-wide strips to make and attach the binding.

ADDING THE EXTRA SHAPES

Refer to the photo on page 18 for placement guidance throughout.

1. Using the patterns on page 70 and cardstock, trace and cut out 12 elongated hexagons and four small hexagon templates. Pin the templates on the wrong side of the selected fabrics. Trace around each shape and cut them out, leaving a ¼"-wide seam allowance all around each shape.

2. Referring to "English Paper Piecing" on page 12, prepare the shapes. Press. Remove the cardstock templates. Appliqué the shapes onto the wall hanging, positioning them on top of the seam intersections.

3. Sew a vintage button at the center of each pair of elongated hexagons. Sew a running stitch around the four hexagons. Using two strands of Rich Wine, sew a cross-stitch in the middle of the four elongated hexagons at the center of the wall hanging.

my blessings
table topper

- -

I love the simplicity of redwork. Contrast between cream and different shades of red exalts the core values expressed in this table topper: the love of a comfortable home, the gratitude for a good harvest stored in the barn, the feeling of faith when walking into a church, and the big dreams of a child growing up and learning in the classroom. So few words with such a great and powerful meaning.

FINISHED TABLE TOPPER: 26" × 26"
FINISHED BLOCKS: 8" × 8"

MATERIALS

Yardage is based on 42"-wide fabric.

Fabrics

¾ yard of cream tone on tone for block backgrounds and setting triangles

¼ yard of red print for border

6 squares, 10" × 10", of assorted red prints for elongated hexagons and center block

12" × 12" square of unbleached muslin for hexagons

4 squares, 2½" × 2½", of assorted cream or light red prints for center block

Black scraps for roof appliqués

⅞ yard of fabric for backing

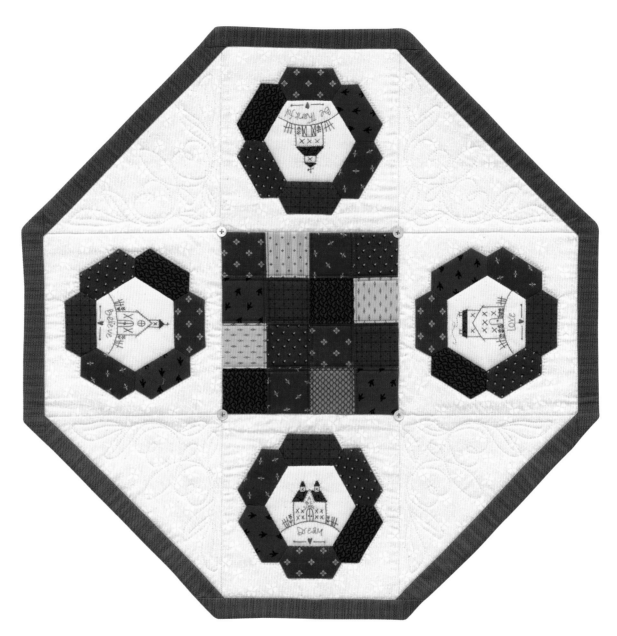

Blocks are shown at actual size on pages 37–40.

Other Materials

30" × 30" square of batting

12" × 12" square of lightweight fusible stabilizer

10" × 10" square of fusible fleece

4" × 6" rectangle of paper-backed fusible web

2 water-soluble appliqué sheets, approximately 8" × 11"

4 vintage buttons, ⅜" diameter

Cardstock

Cotton Embroidery Floss

Color listed is for 6-strand Valdani embroidery floss.

Rich Wine (O507) for embroidery

CUTTING

From the cream tone on tone, cut:

4 squares, 8½" × 8½"

1 square, 12⅝" × 12⅝"; cut into quarters diagonally to yield 4 setting triangles

From the assorted red prints, cut a *total* of:

12 squares, 2½" × 2½"

From the red print for border, cut:

3 strips, 1½" × 42"; crosscut into 8 strips, 1½" × 13"

PREPARING THE HEXAGONS

1. Fuse the stabilizer to the wrong side of the muslin square.

2. Using a light source and the patterns on page 77, trace four hexagon shapes onto the right side of the muslin square, making sure to leave about 1¾" between the hexagons. Using the patterns on pages 75 and 76, trace a different scene in the center of each hexagon.

3. Cut out the hexagons, leaving a ¾"-wide seam allowance all around each shape.

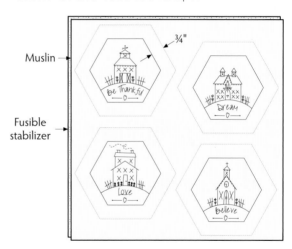

Cut out both layers.

4. Using Rich Wine floss, embroider all lines within the four scenes except for the roofs. All embroidery is stitched using two strands of cotton floss unless otherwise noted.

- **Backstitch:** hilly lines, buildings, chimneys, towers, cross and weather vane, doors and straight handles, windows, fences, and lines on each side of the hearts; words and letters using one strand

- **Satin stitch:** hearts

- **Colonial knot:** round handles, weather vane knob, and dots at end of lines; flowers using one strand

- **Running stitch:** roof underscores and smoke using one strand

- **Lazy daisy stitch:** leaves and stems in one strand

5. Referring to "Fusible Appliqué" on page 11 and using the roof patterns on pages 75 and 76, trace each shape once onto the paper side of the fusible web. Roughly cut out the fusible-web shapes.

6. Place each shape, fusible side down, on the wrong side of the black scraps. Follow the manufacturer's instructions to fuse the shapes to the fabric. Let the fused shapes cool, and then carefully cut them out on the drawn lines. Peel off the paper backing and appliqué the roofs in place.

7. Trace the hexagon pattern on page 77 onto cardstock. Cut out the template exactly on the traced lines. Place the template on the nonadhesive side of the fusible fleece and trace four hexagon shapes. Cut out each shape on the traced line.

8. Using a light source, center the adhesive side of each fusible-fleece hexagon on the wrong side of each muslin hexagon. Following the manufacturer's instructions, fuse the layers together.

9. Quilt along the hilly lines and all around the building shapes.

PREPARING THE ELONGATED HEXAGONS

1. Using a light source and the pattern on page 77, trace 24 elongated hexagons onto the water-soluble appliqué sheets. Cut out the shapes exactly on the lines.

2. Fuse four water-soluble shapes onto the wrong side of each red print. Cut out the shapes, leaving a ⅜"-wide seam allowance all around each shape.

ASSEMBLING THE MEDALLION BLOCKS

1. Referring to "English Paper Piecing" on page 12, use a ladder stitch to join six elongated hexagons and one embroidered hexagon, sewing one side at a time and making sure to maintain the original dimensions. Always check the shapes against the original patterns for accuracy. Knot, but don't clip, the thread at each corner. To travel to an unstitched side, sew a running stitch in the seam allowance only. Knot the thread and then ladder stitch the next side seam.

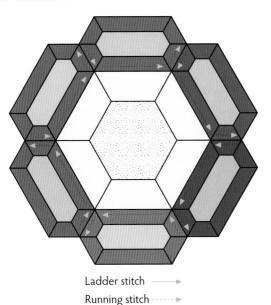

Ladder stitch ⟶
Running stitch ┈┈⟶

2. Center and appliqué each medallion onto the right side of a cream square to make four blocks that measure 8½" square, including the seam allowances.

MAKING THE CENTER BLOCK

Press the seam allowances as indicated by the arrows.

Lay out 12 red and four cream or light red 2½" squares in four rows of four squares each. Sew the squares in each row together. Join the rows to make a block that measures 8½" square, including the seam allowances.

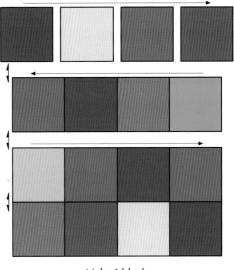

Make 1 block,
8½" × 8½".

ASSEMBLING THE TABLE TOPPER

1. Lay out the blocks and cream setting triangles in three rows as shown in the assembly diagram. Sew the blocks and triangles together into rows. Join the rows to make the table-topper center. Trim the ends of the setting triangles even with the edges of the blocks.

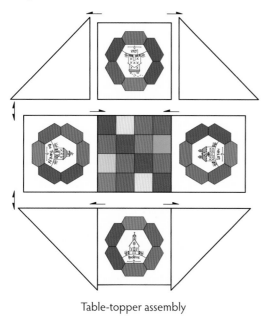

Table-topper assembly

2. Sew a red 1½" × 13" strip to the edge of each setting triangle, right sides together. Press and trim the strips even with the outer edges of the blocks.

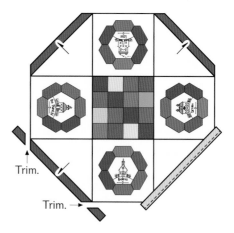

3. Sew a red strip to the edge of each block, right sides together. Press and trim the strips even with the angled sides.

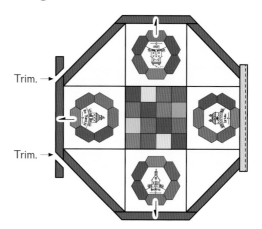

FINISHING THE TABLE TOPPER

1. Layer the table topper on top of the backing, right sides together. Cut the backing even with the outer edges of the top. Place the table topper and backing on top of the batting. Pin the layers together.

2. Sew around the perimeter, leaving about 10" open along the edge of one setting triangle for turning.

3. Trim the batting even with the backing. Turn the table topper right side out through the opening.

4. Press well. Hand stitch the opening closed.

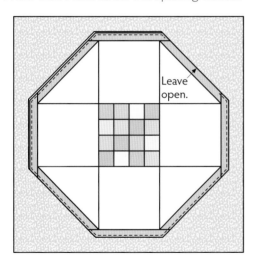

5. Machine or hand quilt. I quilted along both sides of each seam in the center block and in the ditch around the center block, setting triangles, both sides of the elongated hexagons, and the perimeter of the border. A decorative running stitch was used around the medallions, about ¼" from the seamline. The quilting design on page 77 was quilted in each setting triangle.

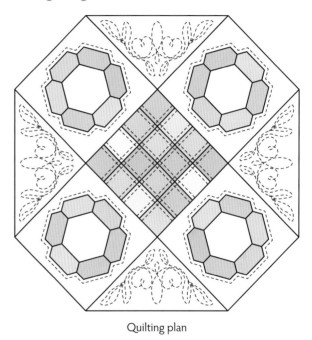

Quilting plan

6. Sew a vintage button to each corner of the center block.

the simple life table runner

It's a typically sunny day in this charming little village dozing on the grassy hills. I've created a scene all about life as it should be—as simple as ABCs and 123s! Lovely apple cores, a little appliqué, and embroidered details give life to this table runner, which could easily be turned into a wall hanging. It's a sweet sampler to remind us that the best things in life are free, and very little is needed for true happiness.

FINISHED TABLE RUNNER: 30½" × 12½"
FINISHED BLOCKS: 8" × 8"

MATERIALS

Yardage is based on 42"-wide fabric. Fat quarters measure 18" × 21". Fat eighths measure 9" × 21".

Fabrics

⅓ yard of beige tone on tone for block backgrounds

¼ yard of cream tone on tone for sashing and border

1 fat quarter of blue print for sky

1 fat quarter of olive green solid for vines, leaves, and hexagons

2 fat eighths of different light green prints for hills

10" × 10" square of charcoal print for petals

Assorted fabric scraps for house, barn, church, school, and tractor appliqués

⅓ yard of charcoal solid for binding

½ yard of fabric for backing

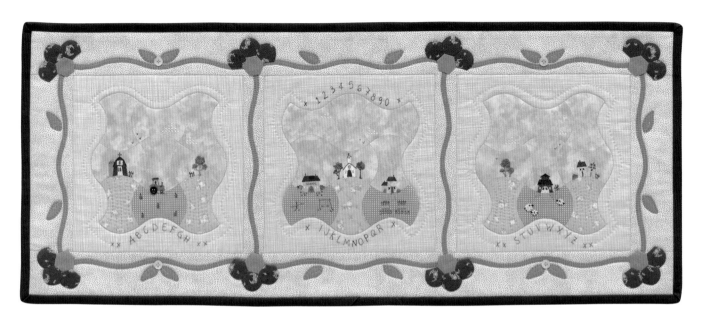

Blocks are shown at actual size on pages 51–53.

Other Materials

17" × 35" rectangle of batting

¾ yard of 12"-wide lightweight fusible stabilizer

⅓ yard of 16"-wide paper-backed fusible web

3 water-soluble appliqué sheets, approximately 8" × 11"

4 vintage buttons, ⅜" diameter

1 brown micro button, about ⅛" diameter

1 brown mini button, ¼" diameter

Black Pigma pen, size 01

Cardstock

Glue pen

Wool Thread

Colors listed are for Valdani wool thread.

Black (W111), size 15, for sheep legs, heads, ears, and tails

Ivory (W400), size 8, for sheep bodies

Ivory (W400), size 15, for clouds

Cotton Embroidery Floss

Colors listed are for 6-strand Valdani embroidery floss.

Black Medium (8112) for barn roof, weather vane, and silo top

Bronze (P9) for seesaw, swing, door, letters, and numbers

Brown (P12) for fences, pumpkin stems, door details, and soil

Distant Grass (M80) for meadows and grass

Forgotten Lavender (H208) for flowers

Heavenly Hue (JP11) for chimney smoke

Nantucket Rose (JP5) for flowers

Old Cottage Grey (O126) for tractor, chimneys, birds, church roof, church cross, and house windows

Olive Green (P2) for grass, foliage, flower stems, pathways, and bushes

Quiet Fall (O534) for pumpkins

Rust (H201) for tree trunk, branches, soil, and door

Rusty Gold (O67) for church windows

Spring Lights (M12) for tractor headlight

Subtle Elegance (M49) for door and window details, barn door details, and barn windows

Tea-Dyed Stone (O178) for swing ropes, grass, and soil

Toffee (O505) for doors

CUTTING

From the beige tone on tone, cut:

3 squares, 8½" × 8½"

From the cream tone on tone, cut:

1 strip, 1½" × 42"; crosscut into 2 strips, 1½" × 8½"
2 strips, 2½" × 42"; crosscut into:
    2 strips, 2½" × 30½"
    2 strips, 2½" × 8½"

From the fusible stabilizer, cut:

3 squares, 8½" × 8½"

From the charcoal solid, cut:

3 strips, 2½" × 42"

PREPARING THE APPLE CORES

1. Trace the apple core pattern on page 74 onto cardstock. Cut out the template exactly on the traced lines.

2. Place the template on the nonadhesive side of the water-soluble appliqué paper and trace 27 apple core shapes. Carefully cut out each shape on the traced line.

3. To make the sky shapes, fuse 18 water-soluble shapes onto the wrong side of the blue print, leaving about 1" between the shapes. Cut out the shapes, adding a ⅜"-wide seam allowance all around the shapes.

4. To make the hill shapes, fuse five water-soluble shapes onto the wrong side of one light green print, leaving about 1" between the shapes. In the same way, fuse the remaining four shapes onto the wrong side of the other light green print. Cut out the shapes, adding a ⅜"-wide seam allowance all around the shapes.

ASSEMBLING THE MEDALLIONS

Refer to "English Paper Piecing" on page 12 as needed. Take care to maintain the original shape, always checking the shape against the original pattern.

1. Clip the seam allowances all around each fabric apple core, stopping a few threads before the traced lines. Clipping makes it easier to fold the seam allowance over the template.

2. Fold the seam allowances over the template and glue them in place.

3. Place two shapes on a flat surface, right side down, and align the curved edges. Use a ladder stitch to join the pieces. Continue in the same way to join six sky and three hill shapes to make a medallion. Make three medallions.

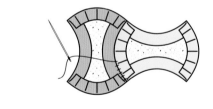

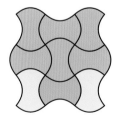

Make 2.

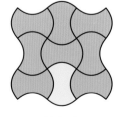

Make 1.

PREPARING THE APPLIQUÉS

Refer to "Fusible Appliqué" on page 11 as needed. Appliqué patterns for each medallion are on page 70; the vine and leaf patterns are on page 74.

1. Trace each of the appliqué shapes for medallions once onto the paper side of the fusible web. Roughly cut out the fusible-web shapes.

2. Trace the vine and leaf shapes the number of times indicated onto the paper side of the fusible web. Roughly cut out the fusible-web shapes.

3. Place each shape, fusible side down, on the wrong side of the appropriate appliqué fabric. Follow the manufacturer's instructions to fuse the shapes to the fabric. Let the fused shapes cool, and then carefully cut them out on the drawn lines. Wait to peel off the paper backing until you're ready to use the fabric shape.

Extra Stitches

To achieve perfectly flat medallions, make a couple extra tiny stitches at the corners of the center apple core on each medallion, making sure to stitch through all the layers. Use a matching thread color and you won't even notice the stitches.

ABC MEDALLION

Referring to the ABC medallion pattern on page 71, appliqué the silo, barn, door, window, and tractor. Mark the rectangles on the barn door and window, and draw the tractor driver's silhouette using a black Pigma pen. All embroidery is worked with two strands of cotton floss unless otherwise noted.

- **Stem stitch:** barn roof in Black Medium, tractor roof and chimney in Old Cottage Grey, and tree trunk and branches in Rust

- **Backstitch:** fences and pumpkin stems in Brown, tractor headlight in Spring Lights, weather vane in one strand of Black Medium, remaining tractor details and birds in one strand of Old Cottage Grey, and grass in one strand of Olive Green

- **Running stitch:** vertical lines on meadows in Distant Grass and detail on silo top in one strand of Black Medium

- **Cross-stitch:** details on door and window in Subtle Elegance and clouds in Ivory wool, size 15

- **Bullion stitch:** pumpkins in Quiet Fall

- **Colonial knot:** chimney smoke from tractor in Heavenly Hue, foliage in Olive Green, and loose soil under the tractor in one strand of Rust

123 MEDALLION

Referring to the 123 medallion pattern on page 72, appliqué all buildings and church and school doors. Mark church windows and the word *School* using a black Pigma pen. All embroidery is worked with two strands of cotton floss unless otherwise noted.

- **Stem stitch:** church roof in Old Cottage Grey and tree trunks and branches in Rust

- **Backstitch:** house fences in Brown, flower stems in Olive Green, chimneys in Old Cottage Grey, seesaw and swing in Bronze; stitch remaining items using one strand: school fences and line dividing school door in Brown, swing ropes in Tea-Dyed Stone, church grass in Olive Green, school grass in Distant Grass, and church cross, window, and birds in Old Cottage Grey

- **Running stitch:** chimney smoke in one strand of Heavenly Hue and pathways in one strand of Olive Green (house) and one strand Distant Grass (school)

- **Cross-stitch:** central meadow in Distant Grass, school windows in Subtle Elegance, church windows in Rusty Gold, house windows in Old Cottage Grey, flowers in Nantucket Rose and Forgotten Lavender, clouds in Ivory wool, size 15

- **Satin stitch:** big house door in Rust and little house door in Toffee

- **Colonial knot:** foliage and bush in Olive Green, school doorknobs and loose soil outside the school in one strand of Brown

XYZ MEDALLION

Referring to the XYZ medallion pattern on page 73, appliqué the buildings, roofs, and barn door. Mark the dark shapes on the barn door using a black Pigma pen. All embroidery is worked with two strands of cotton floss unless otherwise noted.

- **Stem stitch:** tree trunks and branches in Rust

- **Backstitch:** fences in Brown, dividing line on barn door in Subtle Elegance, chimneys in Old Cottage Grey, grass around the barn in one strand of Olive Green, birds in one strand of Old Cottage Grey, and sheep legs in Black wool, size 15

- **Running stitch:** vertical lines on meadows in Distant Grass, chimney smoke in one strand of Heavenly Hue, pathway to barn in one strand of Olive Green, and grass under the sheep in one strand of Tea-Dyed Stone

- **Cross-stitch:** barn windows in Subtle Elegance, house windows in Old Cottage Grey, and clouds in Ivory wool, size 15

- **Satin stitch:** big house door in Bronze and little house door in Toffee

- **Colonial knot:** foliage and bush in Olive Green; loose soil outside the barn in one strand of Tea-Dyed Stone; sheep bodies in Ivory wool, size 8; and sheep heads in Black wool, size 15

- **Lazy daisy stitch:** ears and tails of sheep in Black wool, size 15

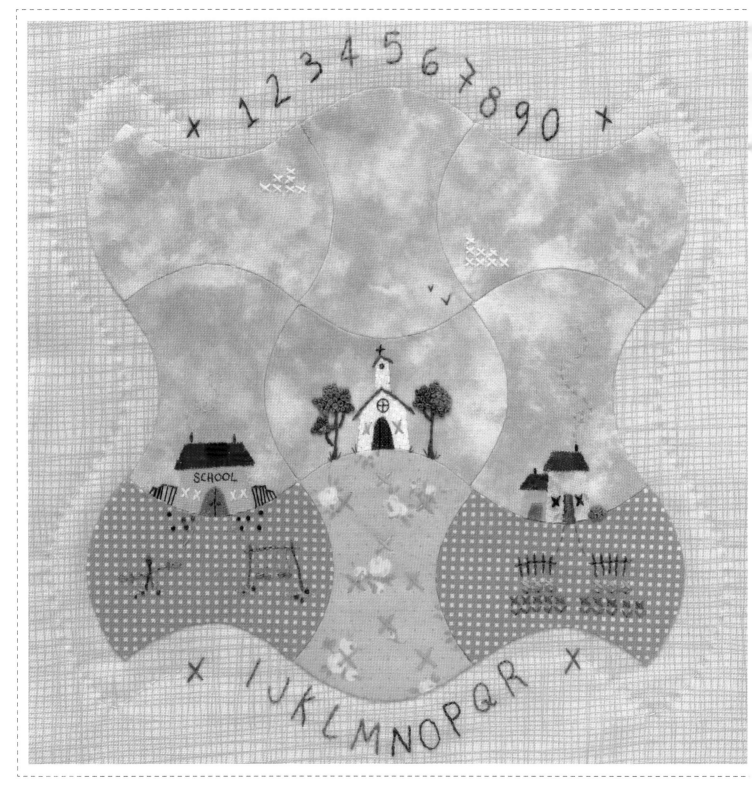

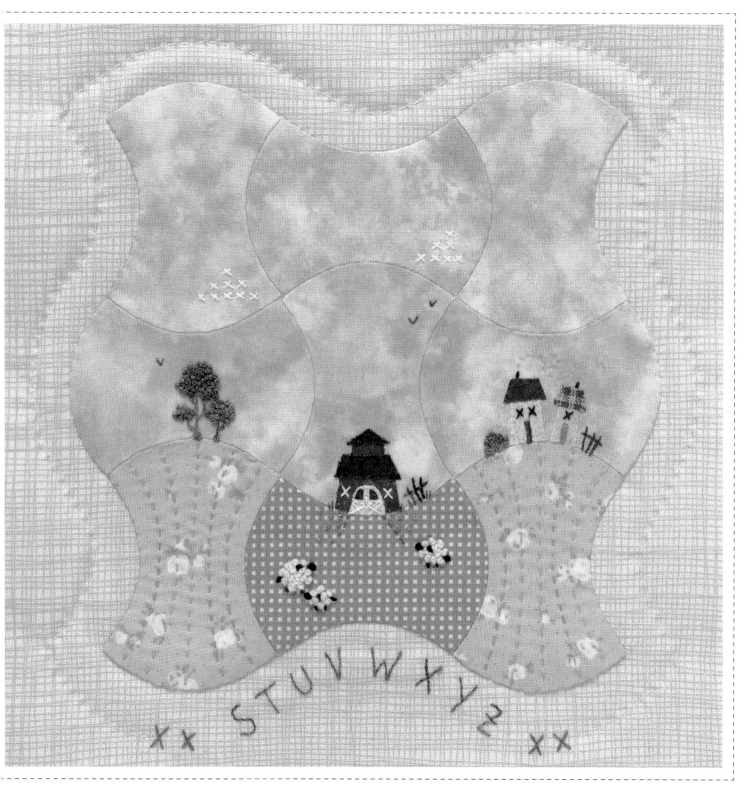

MAKING THE BLOCKS

Refer to the medallion patterns as needed.

1. Fuse a square of stabilizer onto the wrong side of each beige square.

2. Pin or glue each embroidered medallion onto the right side of a beige square. Appliqué the medallions in place.

3. Trace the letters and numbers onto each appropriate block. Backstitch the letters and numbers using two strands of Bronze.

ASSEMBLING THE TABLE RUNNER

Press the seam allowances as indicated by the arrows.

1. Join the blocks and cream 1½" × 8½" strips to make a row that measures 8½" × 26½", including the seam allowances.

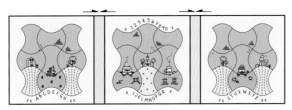

Make 1 row, 8½" × 26½".

2. Sew the cream 2½" × 8½" strips to the short ends of the row. Sew the cream 2½" × 30½" strips to the long edges of the row. Press all seam allowances toward the cream strips. The table runner should measure 30½" × 12½".

ADDING THE SASHING AND BORDER APPLIQUÉS

1. Fuse the olive green vines and leaves in place as shown in the appliqué placement guide on page 55. Finish the raw edges by hand or machine using a blanket stitch. Using a running stitch and two strands of Distant Grass, embroider veins on the leaves.

2. Using a light source and the patterns on page 74, trace 24 petals and eight hexagons onto the nonadhesive side of the water-soluble appliqué paper. Carefully cut out all the shapes on traced lines.

3. Fuse the petal shapes on the wrong side of the charcoal print, leaving about 1" between the shapes. In the same way, fuse the hexagons on the wrong side of the olive green solid. Cut out the shapes, adding a ⅜" seam allowance all around each shape.

4. Fold the seam allowances over the template and glue them in place. Take care to maintain the original shape, always checking the shape against the original pattern.

5. Use a ladder stitch to join the shapes. Knot, but don't clip, the thread at each corner. To travel back to an unstitched side, sew a running stitch in the seam allowance only. Make eight flowers.

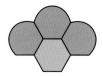

Make 8.

6. Hand stitch each flower in place as shown in the appliqué placement guide.

FINISHING THE TABLE RUNNER

For more detailed information about any finishing steps, visit ShopMartingale.com/HowtoQuilt.

1. Cut the backing fabric 4" larger than the table-runner top. Layer the top with batting and backing. Baste or pin the layers together.

2. Machine or hand quilt. I quilted in the ditch around the three medallions, the perimeter of the blocks, and the vine and flower appliqués. Each medallion is echo quilted about ¼" from the seamline, starting and stopping at the embroidery.

3. Square up the quilt sandwich.

4. Use the charcoal 2½"-wide strips to make and attach the binding.

5. Sew a button to the center of each pair of adjoining leaves. Add the brown mini and micro buttons for the tractor wheels.

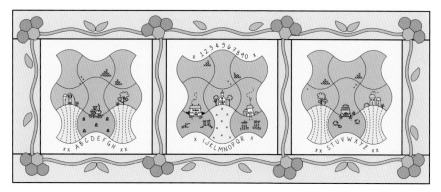

Appliqué placement guide

Beside the Seaside

beseide the seaside pillow

Everybody loves to spend summertime down by the shore. Staring out at the ocean and watching the waves lapping against the sand or seagulls chasing a rolling boat is so relaxing. My seaside scene has been inspired by the charming and chic fishing villages that add such beauty to America's East Coast, where you just might see a lighthouse greeting you with its welcoming beacon.

FINISHED PILLOW: 20" × 20"
FINISHED BLOCK: 8" × 8"

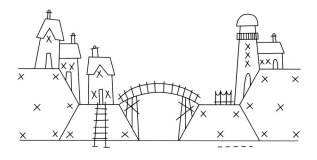

MATERIALS

Yardage is based on 42"-wide fabric.

Fabrics

6" × 6" square of tan solid for mainland

10" × 10" square of blue print for water

10" × 10" square of blue check for sky

⅓ yard of cream solid for center block

Assorted scraps for building and boat appliqués

10 squares, 10" × 10", *total* of assorted navy, red, and cream prints for four-patch units and pillow-back binding (collectively referred to as "medium")

¼ yard of cream stripe for inner border

1½ yards of light solid for pillow-top backing and pillow back

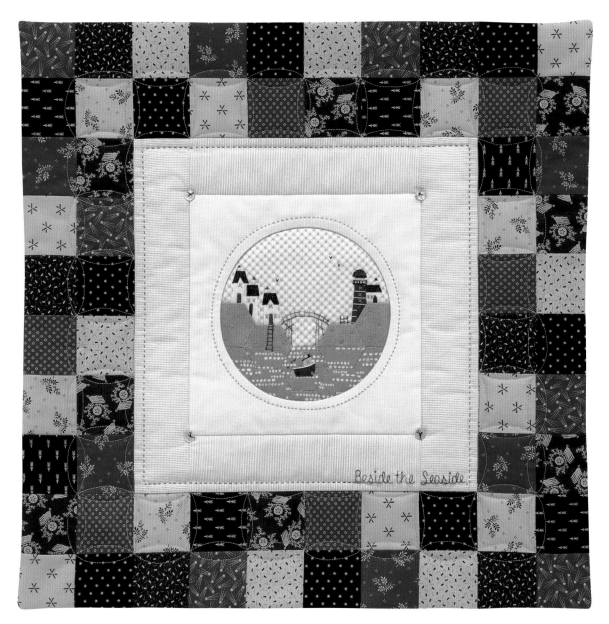

Block is shown at actual size on page 61.

Small Wonders

Other Materials

25" × 25" square of batting

4" × 4" square of paper-backed fusible web

7½" × 9" rectangle of lightweight fusible stabilizer

20" × 20" pillow form

1 water-soluble appliqué sheet, approximately
    8" × 11"

4 vintage buttons, ⅜" diameter

Black Pigma pen, size 01

Cardstock

Cotton Embroidery Floss

Colors listed are for 6-strand Valdani embroidery floss.

Black Medium (8112) for chimneys, lighthouse,
    birds, and boat roof

Bronze (P9) for ladder

Brown (P12) for lighthouse door

Heavenly Hue (JP11) for water

Muddy Pots (JP6) for mainland

Old Cottage Grey (O126) for fence

Rich Wine (O507) for house doors

Rust (H201) for bridge and ropes

Rusty Gold (O67) for boat window

Shaded Brick (O532) for words

Subtle Elegance (M49) for chimneys, handrail,
    and smoke

Toffee (O505) for windows

CUTTING

From the tan solid, cut:
1 strip, 1½" × 5"

From the blue print, cut:
1 strip, 1½" × 5"

From the blue check, cut:
1 square, 7½" × 7½"

From the cream solid, cut:
2 squares, 9" × 9"

From the cream stripe, cut:
2 strips, 2½" × 8½"
2 strips, 2½" × 12½"

From the assorted medium prints, cut a *total* of:
74 squares, 2½" × 2½"

From the fusible stabilizer, cut:
1 square, 7½" × 7½"
1 rectangle, 1½" × 5"

From the light solid, cut:
1 square, 25" × 25"
2 rectangles, 14½" × 20½"

A Smaller Version

To make a finished pillow that measures 16"
square, sew just one row of squares around
the pillow-top center. For the pillow back,
cut two 12½" × 16½" rectangles.

PREPARING THE HEXAGONS

1. Trace the hexagon pattern on page 79 onto cardstock. Cut out the template exactly on the traced lines.

2. Place the template on the nonadhesive side of water-soluble appliqué paper. Trace 10 hexagons. Carefully cut out each shape on the traced line.

ASSEMBLING THE LANDSCAPE

Refer to "English Paper Piecing" on page 12 as needed. Press the seam allowances as indicated by the arrows.

1. For mainland, fuse two water-soluble hexagons onto the wrong side of the tan solid, leaving about 1" between shapes. Cut out the hexagons, adding a ⅜"-wide seam allowance all around the shapes.

2. For the water, fuse six water-soluble hexagons onto the wrong side of the blue print, leaving about 1" between shapes. Cut out the hexagons, adding a ⅜"-wide seam allowance all around the shapes.

3. For mainland and water, join tan and blue strips along one long edge to make a pieced unit that measures 2½" × 5", including seam allowances.

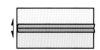

Make 1 unit,
2½" × 5".

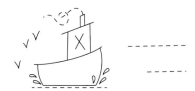

4. Fuse the two remaining water-soluble hexagons on the wrong side of the pieced unit, placing opposite points exactly on the seamline as shown. Cut out the hexagons, adding a ⅜"-wide seam allowance all around the shapes.

Water-soluble hexagons

⅜"

5. Fold the seam allowances over the template and glue in place. Take care to maintain the original shape, always checking the shape against the original pattern.

6. Use a ladder stitch to join the hexagons to make the mainland and water landscape. Knot, but don't clip, the thread at each corner. To travel to an unstitched side, sew a running stitch in the seam allowance only. Knot the thread and then ladder stitch the next side seam.

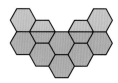

PREPARING THE APPLIQUÉS

Refer to "Fusible Appliqué" on page 11 as needed.

1. Using the appliqué patterns on page 79, trace each shape once onto the paper side of the fusible web. Roughly cut out the fusible-web shapes.

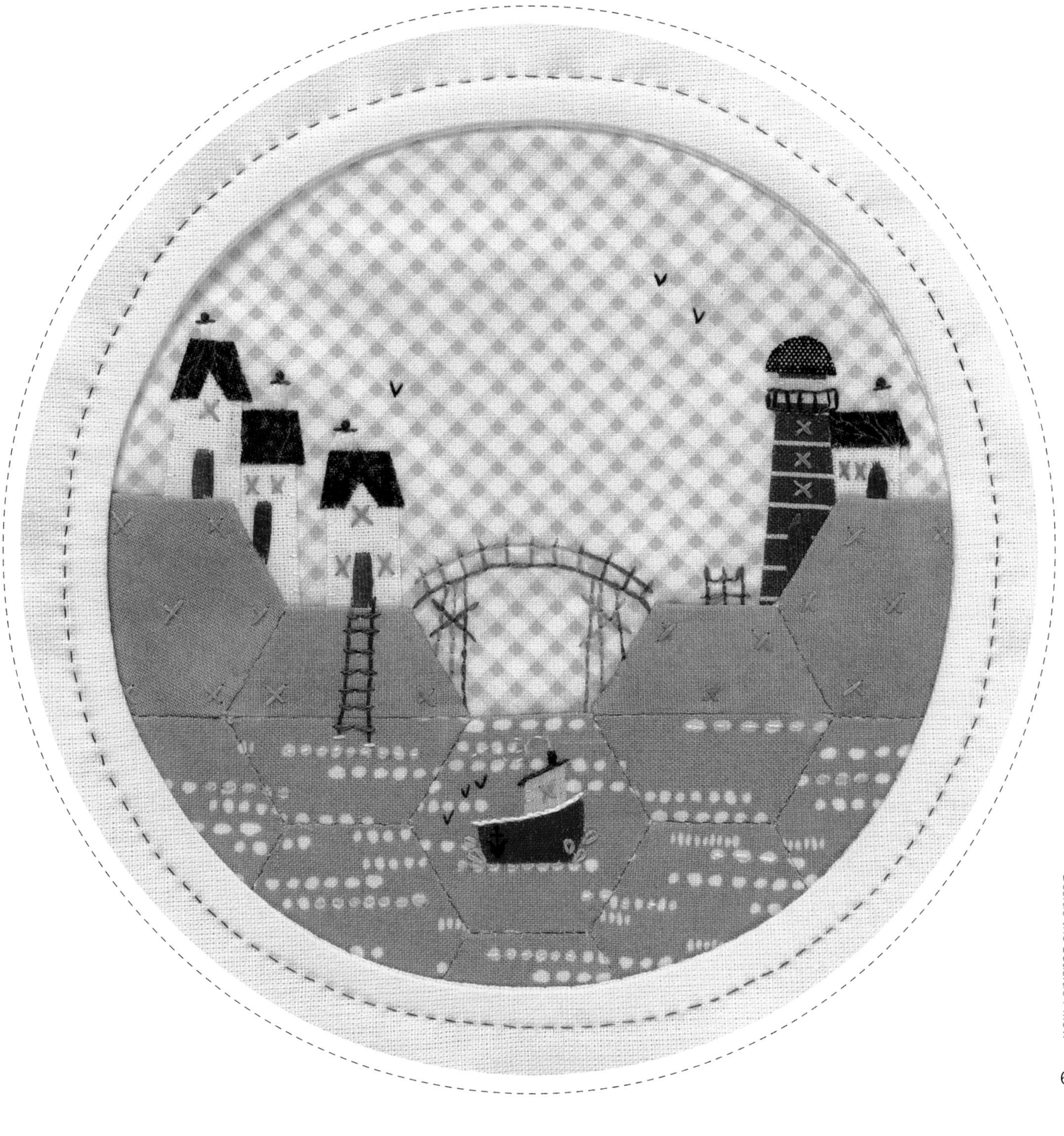

2. Place each shape, fusible side down, on the wrong side of the appropriate appliqué fabric. Follow the manufacturer's instructions to fuse the shapes to the fabric. Let the fused shapes cool, and then carefully cut them out on the drawn lines. Wait to peel off the paper backing until you're ready to use the fabric shape.

EMBELLISHING THE CENTER BLOCK

All embroidery is stitched using two strands of cotton floss unless otherwise noted.

1. Fuse the square of stabilizer to the wrong side of the blue checked square.

2. Using a light source and the landscape medallion on page 78, center and trace the outer circle. Trace the placement of the mainland and water composition and the buildings.

3. Appliqué the buildings and roofs in place. Add embroidery details as follows.

- **Satin stitch:** house doors in Rich Wine, chimneys in Subtle Elegance, and lighthouse door in Brown

- **Backstitch:** chimney details and lighthouse balcony in Black Medium, bridge and ropes in Rust, fence in Old Cottage Grey, and birds in one strand of Black Medium

- **Cross-stitch:** all windows in Toffee

- **Colonial knot:** round chimney details in Black Medium

4. Align the mainland and water composition with the marked line. Appliqué the composition in place.

5. Appliqué the fishing boat. Mark the anchor silhouette using a black Pigma pen. Add embroidery details as follows.

- **Stem stitch:** handrail in Subtle Elegance and roof in Black Medium

- **Satin stitch:** chimney in Black Medium

- **Cross-stitch:** window in Rusty Gold and mainland details in Muddy Pots

- **Backstitch:** ladder in Bronze and birds in one strand of Black Medium

- **Running stitch:** flat waters in Heavenly Hue and chimney smoke in one strand of Subtle Elegance

- **Lazy daisy stitch:** splashing waters in Heavenly Hue

ASSEMBLING THE CENTER BLOCK

1. Using a light source and the landscape medallion, center and trace the outer circle onto the wrong side of one cream solid square.

2. Pin the two cream solid squares right sides together, with the marked square on top. Carefully stitch on the line, sewing slowly and continuously to achieve a perfectly round circle. Press.

3. Cutting through both layers, cut out inner circle, about ⅜" inside the stitched line. Clip the seam allowances. Turn the top square only right side out through the hole. Press carefully. Trim squares to measure 8½" square, keeping the circle centered.

 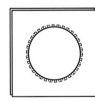

Cut out ⅜" inside   Clip curves.
stitched circle.

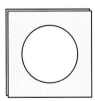

4. Zigzag stitch around the perimeter of the squares, keeping the raw edges aligned.

5. Center and glue the landscape scene beneath the cream squares. Appliqué around cream circle.

6. Trim away the excess fabric from the landscape composition, leaving a ⅜" seam allowance beyond the stitched line.

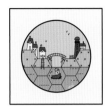

Make 1 block,
8½" × 8½".

ASSEMBLING THE PILLOW TOP

Press the seam allowances in the directions indicated by the arrows.

1. Sew the cream striped 8½"-long strips to the top and bottom of the block. Sew the cream striped 12½"-long strips to opposite sides of the block to complete the inner border.

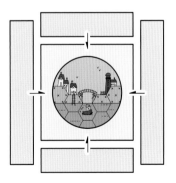

Adding borders

2. Lay out four medium squares in two rows of two squares each. Join the squares to make a four-patch unit. Make 16 units that measure 4½" square, including the seam allowances.

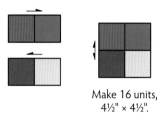

Make 16 units,
4½" × 4½".

3. Join three four-patch units to make a border strip. Make two strips that measure 4½" × 12½", including the seam allowances.

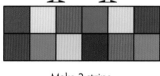

Make 2 strips,
4½" × 12½".

4. Join five four-patch units to make a border strip. Make two strips that measure 4½" × 20½", including the seam allowances.

Make 2 strips,
4½" × 20½".

5. Sew the shorter border strips to opposite sides of the pillow top. Sew the longer strips to the top and bottom of the pillow top. The pillow top should measure 20½" square.

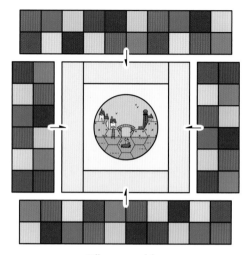

Pillow assembly

6. Referring to the photo on page 58, fuse the rectangle of stabilizer to the lower-right corner of the inner border. Using a light source, trace *Beside the Seaside* on page 79 onto the inner border. Backstitch the words using two strands of Shaded Brick.

QUILTING THE PILLOW TOP

For more detailed information about any finishing steps, visit ShopMartingale.com/HowtoQuilt.

1. Layer the pillow top with batting and the light 25" square. Baste or pin the layers together.

2. Machine or hand quilt. I quilted in the ditch all around the inner circle, the perimeter of the block, and the inner border. Within the inner border, I used two strands of Shaded Brick to sew a running stitch ¼" from the seamline, starting and stopping at the embroidered words. A petal design was quilted in all the squares.

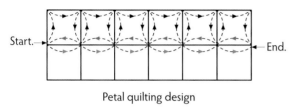

Start. ← → ← End.

Petal quilting design

3. Sew a vintage button on each corner of the center block.

4. Square up the quilt sandwich to measure 20½" square.

FINISHING THE PILLOW

1. To make the pillow back, fold over ¼" on one 20½" edge of a light rectangle, and then fold over ¼" again. Press and machine stitch along the folded edge.

2. Join the remaining 10 medium squares to make a 2½" × 20½" binding strip. Use the pieced strip to bind one 20½" edge of the remaining light rectangle.

3. Overlap the pillow backs from steps 1 and 2, right sides up as shown, to make a 20½" square.

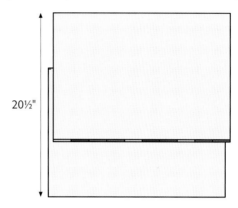

20½"

4. Pin the pillow top on top of the pillow backs, right sides together and raw edges aligned. Sew all around the perimeter using a ¼" seam allowance. Then zigzag stitch around the edges to prevent fraying.

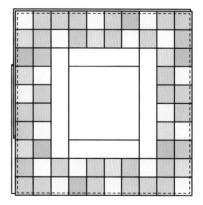

5. Turn the pillow right side out; press. Insert the pillow form through the opening.

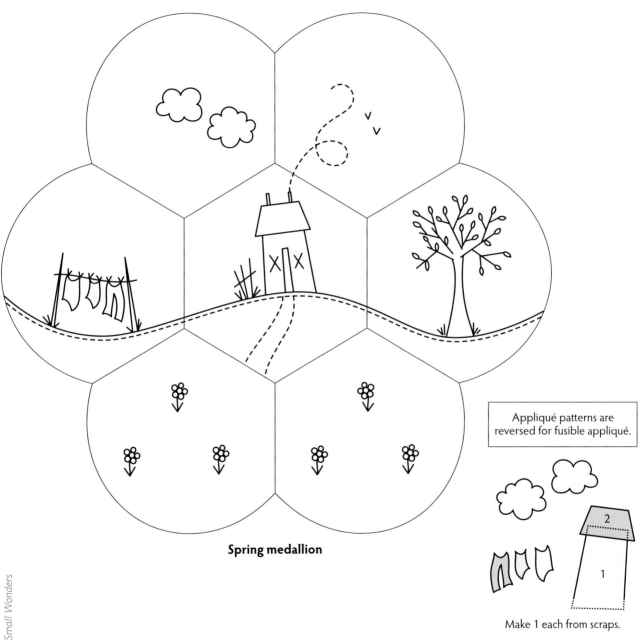

Spring medallion

Appliqué patterns are reversed for fusible appliqué.

2

1

Make 1 each from scraps.

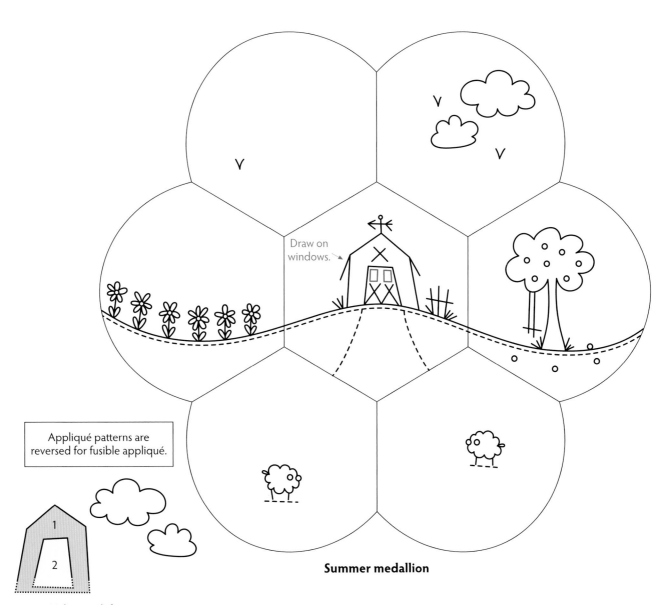

Draw on windows.

Appliqué patterns are reversed for fusible appliqué.

Make 1 each from scraps.

Summer medallion

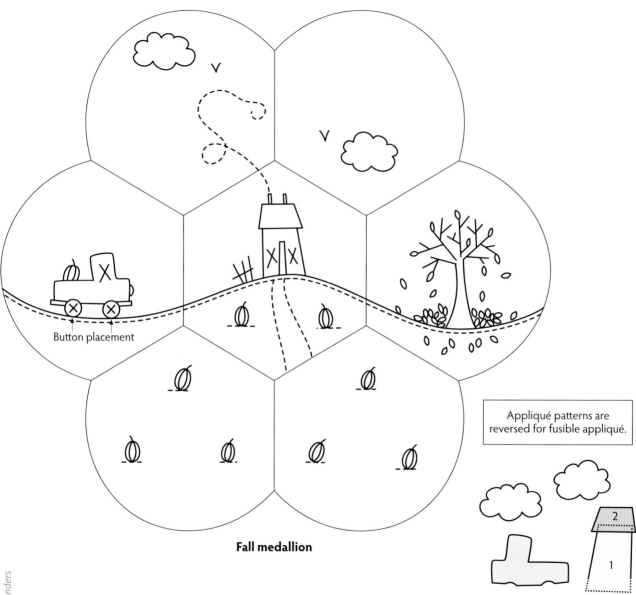

Button placement

Appliqué patterns are
reversed for fusible appliqué.

Fall medallion

Make 1 each from scraps.

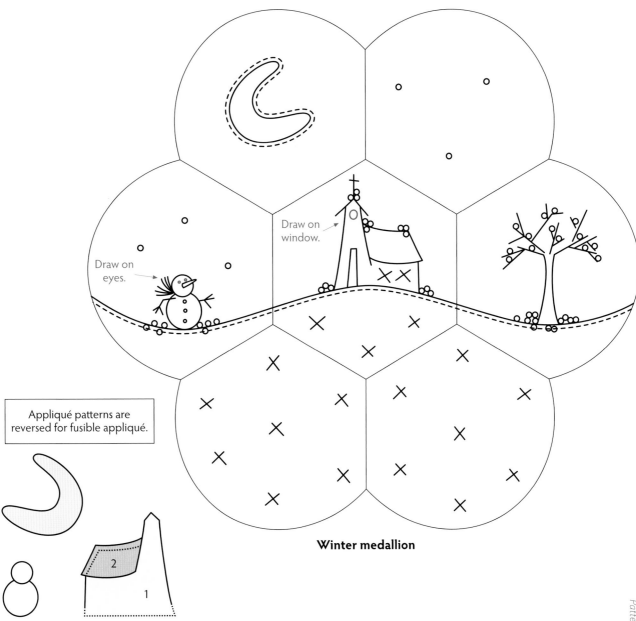

Draw on window.

Draw on eyes.

Appliqué patterns are reversed for fusible appliqué.

Winter medallion

Make 1 each from scraps.

FOUR SEASONS DREAM WALL HANGING

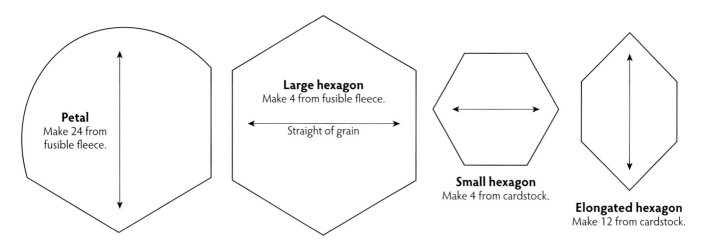

Petal
Make 24 from fusible fleece.

Large hexagon
Make 4 from fusible fleece.

Straight of grain

Small hexagon
Make 4 from cardstock.

Elongated hexagon
Make 12 from cardstock.

THE SIMPLE LIFE TABLE RUNNER

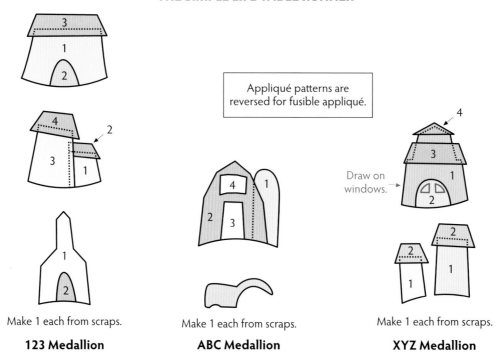

Appliqué patterns are reversed for fusible appliqué.

Draw on windows.

Make 1 each from scraps.

123 Medallion

Make 1 each from scraps.

ABC Medallion

Make 1 each from scraps.

XYZ Medallion

ABC Medallion

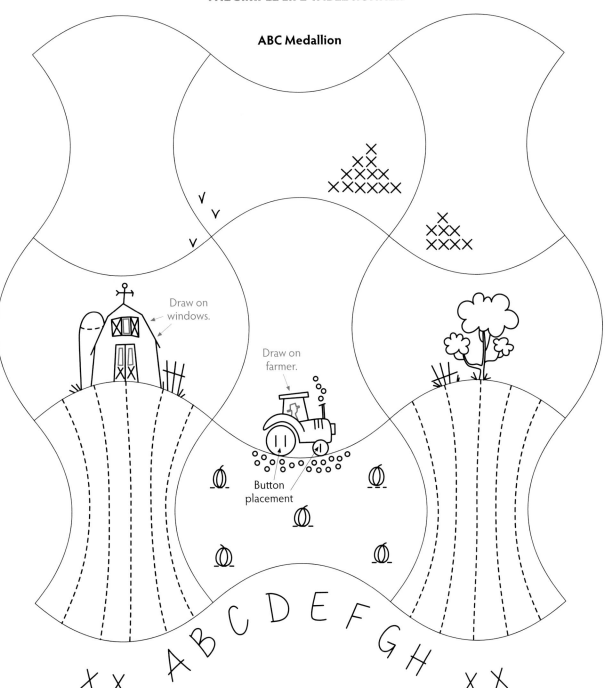

Draw on windows.

Draw on farmer.

Button placement

123 Medallion

X 1 2 3 4 5 6 7 8 9 0 X

Draw on window.

Draw on lettering.

SCHOOL

X I J K L M N O P Q R X

XYZ Medallion

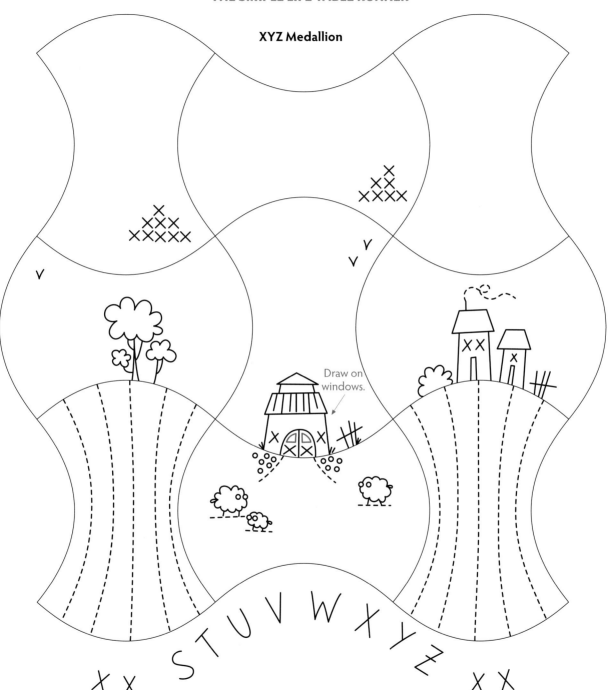

Draw on windows.

Appliqué patterns are reversed for fusible appliqué.

Join to top section along this line.

Apple core
Make 27 from appliqué paper.

Straight of grain

Leaf
Make 8 from olive green solid.

Leaf
Make 8 from olive green solid.

Vine
Make 10 from olive green solid.

Petal
Make 24 from appliqué paper.

Hexagon
Make 8 from appliqué paper.

Join to bottom section along this line.

MY BLESSINGS TABLE TOPPER

Appliqué patterns are reversed for fusible appliqué.

Make 1 each from scraps.

Make 1 from scraps.

Be Thankful

Believe

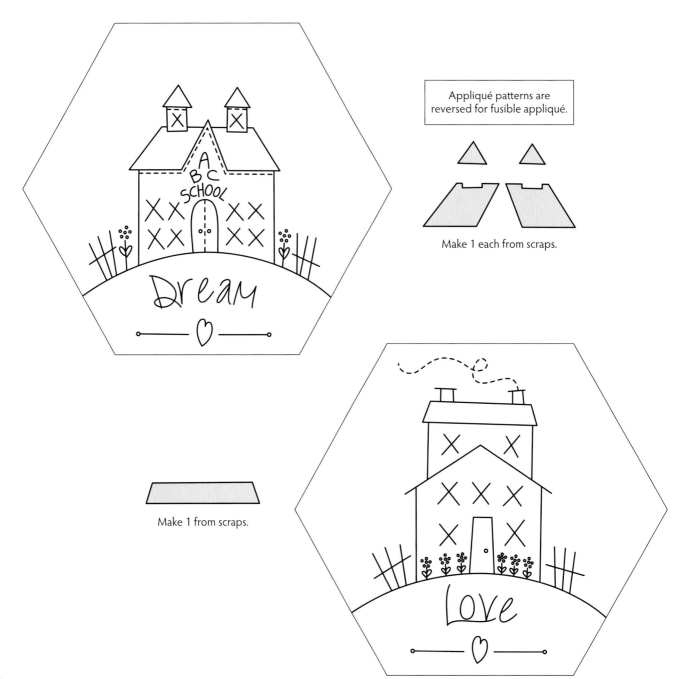

Appliqué patterns are reversed for fusible appliqué.

Make 1 each from scraps.

Make 1 from scraps.

MY BLESSINGS TABLE TOPPER

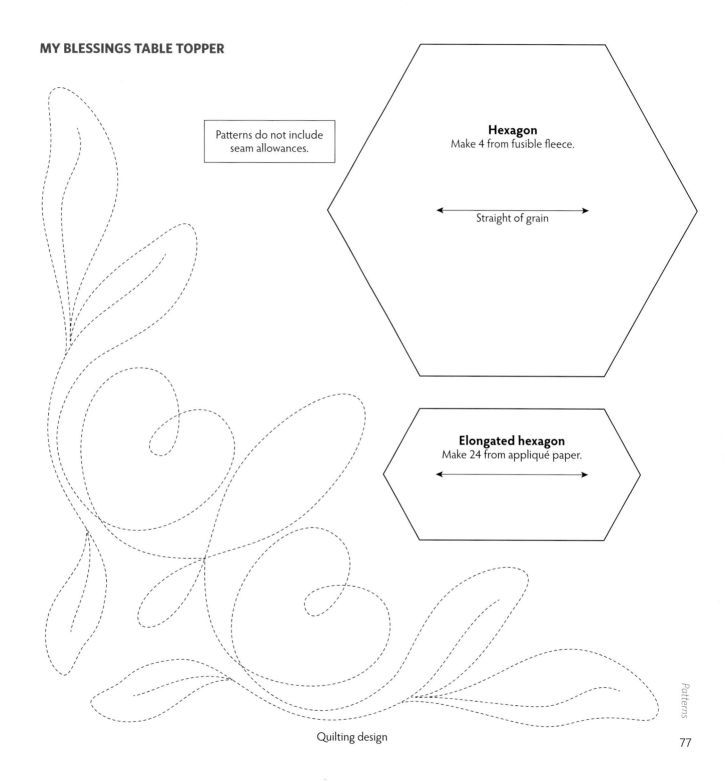

Patterns do not include
seam allowances.

Hexagon
Make 4 from fusible fleece.

←———————→
Straight of grain

Elongated hexagon
Make 24 from appliqué paper.

←———→

Quilting design

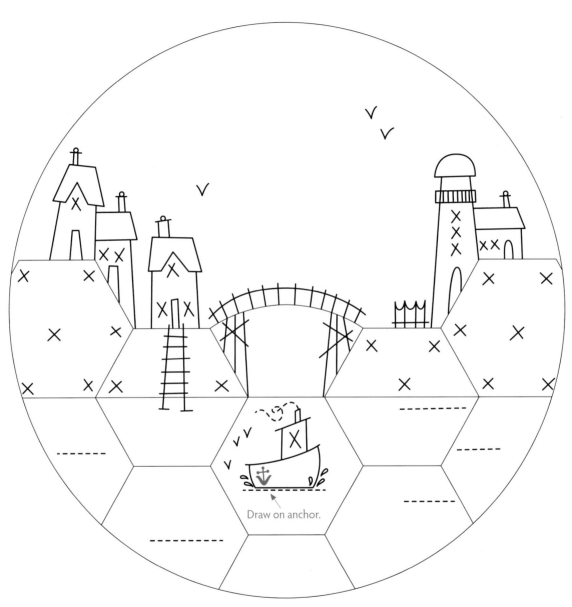

Draw on anchor.

Landscape medallion